What's Hiding Behind Those Ivy Covered Walls?

An Exposé On America's Universities

Joseph S.C. Simplicio Ph.D.

authorHOUSE®

AuthorHouse™
1663 Liberty Drive
Bloomington, IN 47403
www.authorhouse.com
Phone: 1-800-839-8640

First published by AuthorHouse   6/13/2011

ISBN: 978-1-4567-6839-3 (sc)
ISBN: 978-1-4567-6838-6 (hc)
ISBN: 978-1-4567-6840-9 (e)

Library of Congress Control Number: 2011908273

Printed in the United States of America

Dedication

This book is dedicated to everyone who went into the field of education to make a difference and got eaten alive by the system.

Contents

Chapter Twelve

Chapter Thirteen

CHAPTER ONE

INTRODUCTION

Statistics from the United States Department of Education show that there are over 6,500 post secondary institutions of higher education in the United States (2001). The Digest of Education Statistics reports that these institutions enroll more than 19.1 million students. This number is up significantly from the 14.5 million that attended universities and colleges in 1998 (2009).

These institutions include universities, two and four year colleges, non-profit schools, technical and vocational schools, for-profit institutions, and career universities. Some of these schools are public and state funded while others are private, religious based, or corporate owned. These schools vary in size, mission, and vision. On their campuses they tailor their curricula to serve unique, distinctive, and specific populations.

No matter how different these schools are, they all claim to be dedicated to providing a quality education for their students. This education in turn allows these students to better achieve their career goals. Education is after all championed as the pathway to achieving both personal and financial success within the larger community.

Each day nearly 3.6 million individuals including faculty, administrators, staff, and other key campus personnel work diligently in these schools to provide this quality education (The Digest of Education Statistics, 2009). Some are powerful leaders while others are important decision makers. Most though, go about their duties unseen and unheralded. They are the invisible hands that keep the school doors open.

The outside perceptions of these institutions varies, however, there still lingers on the part of many the nostalgic belief that these schools of higher learning are bastions of knowledge where there is an open exchange of informed ideas. Others still see the university as an enclave for wisdom or an oasis for freedom, equality, and fairness.

Many believe that these values insulate those who work within these metaphorically ivy covered walls from petty politics and the influence and corruption of an outside tainted world. Life there is seen as more serene and safer and those who work to shepherd their students' through its hallowed halls answer to a higher calling.

These are wonderfully idealistic views of our nation's universities and colleges.

This book though takes a closer look at these schools from a different perspective, that of an insider who has spent decades plodding through the back corridors of many such institutions in an attempt to make a difference.

It unveils the often harsh realities of campus life for those who have chosen to work at these schools. It discusses campus culture, tradition, and politics. It examines who is hired and why. It explores both the formal and informal bureaucratic hierarchy. It speaks to the leadership within these schools as well as strategies employed to gain professional and personal influence and power. It offers a better understanding of the perspective of those who work there. It also delves into the intricacies of survival and the promises of advancement.

In the end, it provides a candid, unvarnished, and honest look at just what is really occurring on our nation's campuses.

CHAPTER TWO

THE UNIVERSITY CULTURE

Each university has a unique and cherished culture. This culture is born from the institution's history and is steeped in tradition. This tradition in turn reinforces that history and works to incorporate newcomers into the culture by instilling defined cultural values. A university's culture, tradition, and values are not only important, they are vital to the well-being of the institution because they provide stability and continuity.

In order to remain viable though the campus culture must also evolve and adapt to meet change. A university is like a living organism. At times it grows adding new programs, constructing new buildings, and hiring needed personnel. At other times it is forced to modify its focus by shedding obsolete policies, eliminating outdated curricula, and adjusting short term goals. Over time a university matures, and so does its culture. It is important though that the school maintain the core traditional values that define it as an institution.

These core cultural values are kept alive by those long tenured individuals who have dedicated years of service to academia and their university. These are the people who have weathered both the good and bad times. They have watched as the institution grew and changed. They are the keepers of the tradition, the tellers of university tales, and the bedrock of the school's foundation.

Throughout the years they have learned to work together for the benefit of the campus and its students. The interactions that occur amongst and between these individuals is the glue that holds the university together. These interactions create a unique and well-defined chemistry. They set the boundaries for complex relationships.

In order to be successful individuals must learn to understand and work with their colleagues. Administrators must learn to work closely with other administrators in order to develop and implement policies. They must also learn to effectively interact with faculty and staff to ensure that the mission of the institution is fulfilled and that student needs are properly met. Faculty in turn must forge a clear path of cooperation with their colleagues and other university personnel. Added to this mix are the constant interactions between staff, paraprofessionals, and of course students. With so many complex interactions occurring every day on such a grand scale it is easy to understand how the delicate balance of all these interactions can be quickly upset.

The culture of a university with its established traditions and values work to maintain this delicate balance. It provides a set of informal behavioral guidelines. It sets the parameters and monitors for compliance.

In each university there are guardians of the culture who work to maintain it and its delicate balance. They are the keepers of the traditions and protectors of the history and culture of the institution. These individuals include veteran faculty members, entrenched staff members, and others with longevity and seniority. They stand watch over the status quo, they begrudgingly allow only the most necessary of changes, and they usher in newcomers and indoctrinate them into the fold.

In order to be successful within a university one must learn to effectively work with these individuals. Their standing often gives them instant credibility within the campus community. They understand the formal bureaucracy better than anyone and they are the masters of utilizing the informal campus networking system to accomplish their goals. They are the ones who know the "right people" and also know how to get to them. They also know "where the bodies are buried" and how to use this to their advantage. They rarely capitulate to authority and they have the ability to insulate themselves from any real harm.

These individuals can be powerful allies or formidable foes. Garnishing favors from such powerful people can prove quite beneficial in achieving one's professional and personal goals.

The key to effectively dealing with these individuals is to understand their powerbase. They are seen as the "old guard" and their power rests in their small but tight knit unified numbers and in the influential positions they hold within the university as a result of their time spent working there. Others often defer to them because of their senior status. They are rarely questioned when it comes to the history and tradition of the university, especially the oral history of the school. Their recollections of past experiences is accepted almost carte blanche. This deference and acceptance gives them direct input and sway in the decision making process.

In addition, they often hold key positions on the most influential committees. They dominate the Faculty Senate or the Staff Administrative Council and are involved on some level in all crucial decisions that affect the campus and its personnel.

Use of institutionalized formal power is ineffective in dealing with such strong individuals. Therefore, in order to work effectively within this informal hierarchical structure an outsider must acknowledge and understanding all of these factors.

The key is to become one of them. This can be accomplished by "earning one's stripes" through longevity. It can also be accomplished though by slowly immersing oneself into their world. This means volunteering for key committees, offering to help with their pet projects, and most importantly, publicly supporting their causes whenever possible. Although one may not be able to give support at every juncture, until one can gain a powerbase it is important to not be seen as an adversary. Adversaries are dealt with swiftly and the damage caused to one's career or reputation usually cannot be repaired. Like elephants, these individuals have long memories. If opposition must be posed it should be channeled privately through other powerful campus individuals. Even the most solid wall is porous and individuals do have their own agendas. Recognizing and using these factors to one's own advantage is smart.

If the "in group" has one weakness it lies in their belief that they are untouchable. They assume because they are powerful, they will always be powerful. They surmise that by ostracizing and isolating any newcomers who might challenge their interpretation of the school's culture they will remain invincible. This conscious decision to exclude less powerful campus individuals is in the end their Achilles' heel.

These excluded and often forgotten individuals include those who work in less than glamorous positions within the university such as maintenance, facilities, janitorial services, the Information Technology (IT) people, those who are too new to have any influence at all, and those individuals on campus who are viewed as "strange characters."

These individuals may be known as geeks, nerds, freaks, or even the odd balls, but collectively they make up what is known as the "fringe" people. These are the invisible people who go about their day doing their jobs and rarely interacting with anyone outside of their immediate circles. They march to the beat of a different drummer and are seen as peculiar. It is interesting that within an institution that espouses personal and intellectual freedom that those who are "different" in any way are seen as defective and inconsequential.

Acceptance by these groups can usually be accomplished by simply spending time with these individuals, getting to know them better on a professional and personal basis, helping them achieve their goals, and by convincing them that they have worth, and in that worth they have untapped power that just needs a voice. Alone these individual groups wield very little power; however, together and unified they possess the ability to orchestrate critical and sweeping change.

If one can learn to effectively gain the confidence of the powerful and in addition gain the support of these less influential fringe groups, than that individual can acquire influence and power that is far more encompassing and far more reaching than that wielded by any one group alone.

Campus culture is indeed based in tradition; however, because it does evolve and change, it is also fluid. Power can change the culture. This power comes from those who work on the campus.

It is therefore possible to marshal untapped human resources and build an all encompassing personal powerbase through these individuals and then use that base to implement needed change while still honoring the university's rich culture and traditions.

CHAPTER THREE

IT ALL STARTS AT THE TOP: DIVERGENT LEADERSHIP STYLES AND THEIR IMPACT UPON A UNIVERSITY

Everyday across thousands of campuses loyal, hard working, and dedicated educators show up to work hoping to make a real difference in the lives of the students they serve. Little do they know that their dedication and hard work are not enough to ensure success for these students.

Universities throughout the United States are faced with diminishing budgets and growing demands on scarce resources. More has to be done with less. In addition, individual employees need to be motivated to work even harder.

The responsibility of effectively utilizing these resources and motivating these individuals lies with the head of the campus. The "boss" is known by many different names. This individual may possess the title of President, Provost, Vice President, or even Director. This person may govern an entire university or just one campus. The name is inconsequential. What is important is this individual's ability to maintain the academic and financial lifeblood of the institution. An exceptional leader is not only an expert in the areas of budget and finance, but also one who can motivate and rally the troops when the wolf is at the door.

These Chief Executive Officers vary greatly in regards to their management style. This style though is pivotal in setting the tone for the school's culture.

Although leadership styles may vary all of these administrators share one common trait. Even though they report to Boards of Trustees or superiors up the line they are in reality the most powerful individuals on their respective campuses. How they wield this power determines the fate of those under their authority. This power can be effectively utilized to the benefit of the school and its people or greatly abused for personal gain and power.

Styles of Leadership

Shared Governance: The Democratic Model

Some leaders work on a shared governance belief. They include others in the ultimate decision making process. They encourage feedback, innovation, and creativity.

This style of management offers many benefits. For example, individuals working under this type of cooperative management style are often enthusiastic and willingly take on additional new assignments and responsibilities. They do so because they believe in the shared vision that they helped create. They have a sense of ownership and pride as a result.

Working in such an environment fosters both professional and personal growth. It works to build confidence in people's abilities to do their job. As Sam Walton points out "outstanding leaders go out of their way to boost the self-esteem of their personnel. If people believe in themselves, it's amazing what they can accomplish" (2010, p.1). This is essential to growth within any university.

This style of leadership also allows for new grass root ideas to filter to the top and encourages change for the betterment of a university.

On the negative side, what the leaders of such institutions sacrifice is ultimate power. Many believe it is worth the cost.

Hands Off: The Laissez Faire Model

The Laissez Faire leadership style was first identified in a major study conducted by Lewin, Lippitt, and White in 1938. Leaders who utilize this style make the choice to allow subordinates to handle the day to day operations of an institution. These leaders focus their attention on only the big picture.

There are obvious advantages and disadvantages to this leadership style.

On the positive side, this strategy permits supervisors to run their areas of responsibility with little interference. Being the experts within these areas they are free to make decisions that affect programs as well as individuals within their realm of influence.

On the negative side, when the administrators deal only with predominately high level priority issues they often lose touch with those they govern. They sacrifice the day to day interactions and networking paradigms that make the school viable. As such they cannot provide effective feedback to faculty and staff in order to improve their job performances.

A second disadvantage is the possibility that with too much power some supervisors will use it to benefit their own personal agendas. This works to the detriment of a university since these supervisors do not see or understand the bigger picture and as such are only concerned with their own departmental needs.

The Micro-Manager: The Autocratic Model

Micro-managers are administrators who believe it is essential to be involved with every aspect of the daily running of an educational institution. There is no task too small for them to oversee. They may delegate, however, they are constantly double checking to make sure their orders are being carried out, and carried out the way they dictate.

These individuals are often self proclaimed experts in every aspect of running a university. Their ideas and their experiences are the only viable ones and those under them soon come to realize that in order to accomplish even the simplest of initiatives they must first have the leader's support. As a result, this autocratic style of leadership discourages creativity and innovation.

Micro-managers do so for a variety of reasons. Some have trust issues. As such they believe they must control everything in order to guarantee success. Others fear personal failure and so transfer the risk of this to others and then take ownership of their work if they are successful. Still others confuse authority with ability and believe in their own superiority.

Whatever the cause the reality is that this style of leadership is counter intuitive. In fact, "it is the opposite of leadership" (Changing Minds, 2010, p.1).

Working under the authority of a micro-manager is grueling and those under such a leader are often tired and frustrated at their inability to accomplish anything.

The Rule Follower: The Bureaucratic Model

Anyone who has spent any real time within a university has met, and probably worked with or under, those individuals who choose to lead strictly by following the rules. These are the "by the book" people. They are quite versed on both policies and procedures as formally established by higher authority. They rarely deviate from the prescribed norm and are reluctant to make any exception that would take their department outside the realm of normal day to day operations.

These are the type of leaders who do not believe in any form of risk taking. To them taking risks opens up the real possibility of failure. Failure in turn could result in problems for their department and more importantly for their own careers. These types of leaders understand that following the rules cannot get them into any trouble at all. They are the "no, we cannot do that" people on campus. Sadly, these leaders become masters in "...the art of making the possible the impossible" (Salcedo, p.1).

While it is true that it is important for individuals to follow well established and time proven policies and procedures to ensure the smooth operation of a university, it is also true that adhering too closely to "the letter of the law" regarding these rules results in inertia. Working under the authority of such individuals stymies innovation, creativity, and both personal and institutional growth. Polices change slowly and as such it is critical for individuals to think "outside the box" in order to meet ever changing times. Doing so under an individual with this leadership style is often difficult or even impossible at times.

The Tyrant: The Fear Model

Tyranny in this world is not dead or exclusively the domain of third world dictators. It lives on many campuses throughout the country. Leaders who possess ultimate power are sometimes tempted to use this power for their own personal gain.

Individuals who utilize this strategy often rule though fear. The belief is that if everyone is afraid, whether it is of losing one's position, or of retaliation, or even making a bad decision, they can be more easily manipulated and controlled.

This style of leadership creates a culture where supervisors, staff, and faculty alike second guess every decision they wish to make. No one wants to make a mistake, so as a result little gets done independently of the leader.

This style of leadership also creates "the emperor has no clothes" mentality. Few are willing to openly challenge any decision made by the leader and those who do are often fired, thus reinforcing the belief on the part of others that it is much better to simply remain silent, even when they know that a bad decision has been made.

Often this type of leader will place people into positions of authority based more upon loyalty than on their expertise, experience, or even abilities. The results can be devastating to a university.

Interestingly enough this style of management is just ineffective by any standard. This is clearly confirmed by the White Stag Leadership

Development group that provides cutting edge training programs for today's leaders when it states that "...authoritarian styles of leadership are less and less responsive to the complex challenges facing society today" (Sharing Leadership, p.1).

As David Antonioni states, "The best and most mature leadership is about selfless service, not about gaining power and control over people" (2010). These leaders do not understand this concept.

Leaders who utilize this style of governance in essence prey upon their employees. They are academic bullies. They accept all the accolades when things go well and publicly blame others when they fail. It is quite obvious that under such circumstances little creativity will exist or be encouraged. As a result the school does not grow until these types of leaders eventually move on to other educational institutions where they can again trumpet their own agendas for personal gain.

The Charismatic Leader: The Inspirational Model

At the other end of the spectrum from the tyrant stands the charismatic leader. Whether it be John F. Kennedy inspiring a nation, Martin Luther King Jr. leading a social movement that revolutionized society, or the President of a small university somewhere in the Midwest, certain individuals have the innate ability to motivate people beyond what they believe they can accomplish.

These types of leaders are quite rare. They understand how to utilize the system for the benefit of their goals and the needs of the institutions they lead. They have mastered the bureaucratic nuisances and subtleties that allow them to effectively achieve these goals.

More importantly, they understand people. They know how to "work a room." They also understand the value of inspiring others. "They pay attention to the person they are talking to at the moment, making that person feel like they are, for that time, the most important person in the world" (Communication-skills-4-confidence, p.1).

These leaders build strong loyal followings and are therefore able to ask more of others who willingly go above and beyond what is expected of them. People just genuinely enjoy working for such individuals and are willing to work harder for them.

Some charismatic leaders are skilled educators who have worked their way up the ranks and have learned a great deal along the way. They truly understand the educational issues that can plague a university and its people. Their knowledge, experience, and ability to persuade others are valuable and powerful tools in making changes and accomplishing goals.

Others who do not possess this type of experience are still able to motivate others who do possess needed expertise. They too can be very effective leaders as a result.

The bottom line is that these types of leaders are able to accomplish a great deal as long as they are not tempted to push their own personal agendas to enhance their own careers.

Conclusion

As can be seen, varying leadership styles can create different campus cultures and consequently achieve different levels of success or failure.

In the end, it is quite clear that the individual at the top who holds the power and makes the final decisions determines the success or failure of the institution and those that work for it.

When all is said and done, it comes down to the reality that leaders who respect and value those who work under them help create a nurturing environment and a culture for success while bad bosses who make bad decisions wreak havoc.

CHAPTER FOUR

NEW IDEAS THAT ARE ACADEMICALLY SOUND ARE GOOD, THOSE THAT BRING IN MONEY ARE EVEN BETTER

<u>Valet Parking on Campus:</u>

<u>An Academically Sound Idea or Just a Good Way to Bring in Needed</u>

<u>Funding?</u>

One of the latest trends on university campuses across the nation is the introduction of valet parking for students. On some campuses the enterprise is run through the Student Affairs office while at others outside vendors are hired. When Student Affairs is involved club members volunteer and portions of the proceeds are filtered back into the clubs based upon participation. The university usually assumes the general liability. On the other hand universities who choose to use outside vendors often pass the cost on to the student body through an activity fee.

Either way, proponents of this endeavor claim that it produces both academic and financial benefits for the school and the students.

On the academic side it is argued that the introduction of this practice will work to counteract tardiness in the classroom, especially for early morning classes. Now that students can simply pull up and drop their cars off to an attendant there is no longer a need on their part to search for parking spots that are often rare on larger campuses. The result is that the chronically late student will no longer be missing valuable class time. Educators anticipate that more class time will result in a better mastery of the course material which in turn will result in higher grades and a better overall Grade Point Average.

In addition, it is argued that those students involved in the running of the valet parking enterprise receive real world experience. They learn important business skills. Students learn how to process credit cards, how to effectively supervise employees, and how to operate a viable business on a daily basis. These give the students practical real life experience in budgeting, marketing, customer relations, and problem solving areas. Classroom theory in essence is put into practice as a result.

On the financial side valet parking works to offset fixed university administrative expenses. The additional income coming into the university can be funneled back to the students directly and their needs can be better met with little or no expense to the university.

Properly publicized this venture can create spin off enterprises that benefit the school and the students alike. Tee shirts with university logos or boldly printed images that espouse such messages as "stay in school" can be given, or better yet, sold to those students who purchase the service.

On the downside the university will have to deal with complaints about missing personal possessions left in the vehicles and damages caused as a result of parking accidents. All in all though many universities believe the benefits far outweigh the problems that might arise and as a result many schools are implementing the practice.

It all sounds good. Costs to students are relatively low running from $5 an hour to $20 a day. There are identifiable academic and financial incentives for implementing valet parking and it seems like a win/win situation for students and administration alike.

Or is there something else happening here?

No one can credibly argue with the reality that even though universities are seen as the bastions of knowledge and the gatekeepers for career success, it is just as factual that they are also business enterprises as well. Be they public, non-profit, or commercial for-profit institutions of higher education, they all have a financial bottom line that has to be met. In the end the books have to balance out. Although faculty may look away or speak in hushed tones about this widely known secret, administrators have understood its reality for years. To meet expenses some of the larger institutions rely on endowments from alumni and friends of the university as well as other initiatives.

In order to reconcile the ever growing need for funding with the mission to provide quality education, many universities have looked to implement money making ideas that have at least a semblance of academic quality. They have done this for decades.

Very often these funds come from areas that are not related at all to academia. The most obvious of these include big time sports programs at some of the most prestigious universities in the nation. While these institutions may assert that their athletes perform at high academic levels and that their graduation rates mirror the general student population, the reality is that successful sports programs, especially those that produce a national championship, are important because they pour millions of dollars into the university coffers. A lucrative football television contract, such as the fifteen year deal given to the Southeastern Conference by CBS can put a university in the black financially for years. It is no accident that "March Madness" is embraced by both the major television networks and universities alike. It produces millions of dollars that are shared across the business and academic worlds jointly.

Although these programs produce valuable student scholarships that provide funding for students who would not otherwise be able to afford higher education, a great portion of the money is also used to fortify the infrastructure of the universities themselves. The number of new buildings that have been constructed and paid for by sports programs on campuses across the nation attests to that fact. In addition, those universities that are successful in sports are able to recruit gifted athletes who in turn provide increased opportunities for continued success in the sports arena. Success breeds more success, and more success can be turned into dollars. It is little wonder then that so many head coaches are paid far more than even the presidents of the universities. In the public sector for example the average salary for a university president is $436,111 and in the private sector it is $358,746 (Jerema, 2010, p.1).

This pales in comparison to the salaries of head coaches at major universities. Jeff Tedford the football coach at the University of California for example, has a guaranteed annual contract of $2.8 million (Wieberg, Upton, Perez, & Berkowitz, 2009, p.1). He is one of twenty five head coaches making at least $2 million each year including Southern California's Pete Carroll who earns over $4 million annually.

The average salary for a football coach at a top 120 school is $1.36 million. Very often even assistant coaches outpace their presidential counterparts. Monte Kiffin, defensive coordinator at Tennessee earns $1.2 million annually (Wieberg, Upton, Perez, & Berkowitz, 2010, p.2).

Tennessee's nine assistant coaches average more than $369,000 a year (Wieberg, Upton, Perez, & Berkowitz, 2009, p.2).

Even more surprisingly, the average university president's salary is increasing by only 2.3% (Jerema, 2010, p.1) compared to coaches' salaries at the major schools that rose 28% in 2009 and 46% since 2007 (Wieberg, Upton, Perez, & Berkowitz, 2009, p.1).

The discrepancies are even more striking when the salaries of coaches are compared to those of full professors who hold a doctorate degree. As Wieberg, Upton, Perez, & Berkowitz point out, these faculty members average $115,509 in comparison (p.2).

These are sobering numbers in light of the massive increases in tuition that university students have witnessed during this time of economic crisis where state appropriations have shrunk, budgets have been drastically cut, and universities have been forced to cut spending, and layoff full-time faculty and staff members. Many of the nation's institutions of higher learning raise tuition an average of 10% each year, while several increase it by 15% or more (Block, 2007, p.1).

Even though individuals such as Hodding Carter, a former assistant Secretary of State for public affairs under president Jimmy Carter, and now a faculty member at North Carolina contends that such practices "...call into question the commitment of much of the institutional leadership in higher education" (Wieberg, Upton, Perez, & Berkowitz, 2009, p.2). The bottom line is that the coaches and their teams bring in more money than university presidents or faculty, and as such, their rewards are substantially higher.

Sports are not the only means for universities to raise needed capital. Very often the universities will turn to outside companies for research funding that can bring in millions of dollars. The University of Colorado at Denver for example received $374 million to fund one thousand, seven hundred and ninety nine research grants in 2006 alone ("UCD Research Dollars Hit a Record $374 Million for FY 2006," 2007, p.1).

While some experiments may call ethical standards into question and concerns may arise about their validity or purpose, the justification is simple for the institutions. From their point of view these research dollars make it possible for major breakthroughs in science or health that could pay real dividends in helping to improve the human condition.

Sometimes this is indeed the case. Even when it is not the case though, what these research dollars do on a regular basis is to help sure up the balance sheets of the universities.

Sports teams and research grant funding are two of the more obvious and public means for universities to raise money. Some smaller schools though do not have the ability to field a championship team or win millions of dollars in research grant money; however, they too can be creative in their fund raising skills. Be it pep rallies, local fundraisers, auctions, or even bake sales, their focus is the same as the larger universities, and that is to secure additional needed funds to keep the institutions' doors open.

Valet parking is but the latest example of that creativity. The concept itself is not new. There has always been valet parking at prestigious restaurants and recently the service has been added to numerous other establishments including hospitals and even funeral homes. Valet parking on campuses is just a further extension of this concept.

It is seen, in the words of the president of High Point University, Nido Qubein, as a way to "...provide a better student experience" (Eisen, 2009, p.1). High Point has a reputation for programs that tend to pamper their students in ways other institutions of higher education do not, including free ice cream, concierge service, and a giant hot tub. Administrators at High Point hope that all of these efforts, including valet parking, will increase the persistence rates at the school and translate into more tuition dollars in the long run.

Qubein is not alone. Valet parking has been implemented in other universities including Florida International University, the University of Southern California, and even Colombia University. Others, such as Florida Atlantic University are seriously considering instituting the service.

Always creative in finding ways to parlay one good money making idea into another several universities such as California State Sacramento have offered students who wish to park their own cars parking lots that are closer to the main buildings for a smaller fee. Still others have added car washing to the menu. Students can now get to class on time and have their cars returned to them shiny clean.

Not everyone though concedes that the idea is a good one. "I've asked many colleagues and they think it's absolutely absurd. Is this an academic institution or a club on South Beach?" (Eisen, 2009, p.2) asks one faculty member while another asks "How about building a new parking garage or making more spots for us" (Eisen, 2009, p.2).

Ben Eisen asks "…Isn't a university supposed to be a young person's last chance to master effective time-management before they get into the 'real world'" (2009, p.3). He laments that "Whatever university students are learning in their classes the lessons they take away from this valet-stand 'curriculum' might be the ones that stick with them after graduation—and that's troubling" (Eisner, 2009, p.3).

The hard core reality is that even in difficult economic times there is still a market for the service. The timing for utilizing this service is in fact perfect. It is being offered to a generation of students who have been catered to throughout their lives on all levels by almost everyone from OnStar helicopter parents to educators. This is a generation that truly feels entitled and this is but one more such entitlement. As Eisner points out there are still plenty of students willing to pay for the opportunity "to live an Entourage lifestyle while earning a degree" (Eisner, 2009, p.3).

Sadly, understanding this fact makes it quite clear that ideas such as valet parking which surface within the academic sector do not always have to offer benefits that support academically sounds practices as long as they are a means to bring in funds for a university.

Chapter Five

The Red Tape Bureaucracy!

"The opera ain't over until the fat lady sings." So said Ralph Carpenter. Although he uttered these now famous words during a Texas Tech university basketball game in March of 1966, it is still applicable today to our modern universities where little, if anything, can be accomplished without first completing the proper paperwork.

Within the entrails of every university exists a hidden bureaucracy. Within this bureaucracy exists the ever present and well known "paper trail." Working in tandem together they lay in wait to claim their victims as they erect obstacles that at times seem insurmountable.

The Form

The *"Great Hall of Paper"* as it is known and feared by many, is the depository for all university records and archives. It uses the dreaded "*form*" as its chief weapon of mass destruction. *Forms* have to be completed continuously throughout the daily work process. Not only do they have to be completed, they have to be completed in the proper manner, and at the proper time.

There are *forms* for everything within the university system. *Forms* for employment, *forms* to order supplies, *forms* to maintain your benefits, *forms* when you are ill, *forms* for security purposes, *forms* for expenses, *forms* for maintenance, *forms* for computer issues, *forms* for room requests, *forms* for events, *forms* to determine who can best assist you, *forms* to instruct you on which *forms* to use, and even *forms* to order more *forms.*

Forms come in different shapes and different lengths, and even different colors. The array is dizzying as is the confusion over which *form* to use at times. It is vital though that one selects and properly completes the correct *form*. If the wrong *form* is utilized, or if it is completed incorrectly, or even if it is processed through the wrong channels, the result can be extensive delays to any project.

What makes the whole process even more daunting is the fact that these *forms* change periodically, often without notice. Filling out requests on outdated *forms* means not only delays, but the inevitability of having to make the original request again, but this time on the new and updated *form,* and this task has to be accomplished no matter how frustrating or how much work it entails. There are no acceptable alternatives.

It is impossible to measure the amount of personnel time that is devoted to completing the *form*, however, universities are unable, or unwilling, to exist without them.

The Right Person

Once one successfully identifies and masters the proper *form* for the task at hand, it must then be submitted to the proper individual in charge of that particular *form*. These individuals are known as the "*keepers*" of the *form*. That is their responsibility and they take it seriously. Their positions depend on it.

Those in charge of the *Great Hall of Paper* and its *forms* are tasked with the responsibility of watching over and guarding the whole process. As a result, they acquire power from the process itself. Understanding that their power is rooted in the daily compliance and enslavement to the proper filing of paper within their particular areas where they are the experts, these individuals guard their *forms* like newborns. Interestingly enough, they are not concerned with the content of the *form*, only the proper utilization of the *form* itself. As such, transgressions are dealt with severely.

To make matters even more complex, at times simply filing the proper *form* is not in itself sufficient. When problems arise, it is necessary for one to go to the *keepers* of the paper and meet with them directly. The key though is to determine which *keeper* must be seen and then arrange a meeting time that is acceptable for that *keeper*.

Once there, it is vital to get the *keeper* to understand what is needed as quickly as possible. This is often not an easy task because the *keepers* are adept at dividing their time and attention between multiple tasks. One's pleas for help are often sandwiched in between telephone calls, outside interruptions, and the daily work of the *keepers*.

Besides dividing their attention among many tasks, the *keepers* also like to play what is known as the "you'll have to see…" game. This they employ on those occasions when it appears that the problem is either just too time consuming or too difficult for a particular *keeper* to handle.

According to the rules of this game, after the needs are explained in great detail, and the *keeper* determines that a *form* cannot be utilized to solve the problem, the *keeper* then ponders the situation and raising an eyebrow in scorn declares that "you'll have to go see (name of *keeper*) about this issue. That person is the only one who can help you." With that said, the *keeper* is free to attend to other duties. Problem solved, at least for the *keeper*.

When this occurs one is forced to find that new *keeper*, arrange an appointment at the *keeper's* convenience, and plead the case in excruciating detail all over again.

The beauty of this game is the ease in which *keepers* can pass the problem off, over, and over again. The result is frustration and anger. These though are counterproductive since the more frustrated and angrier one becomes the less likely one will be to present the case properly. Often as a result, rambling and confusion set in. This can be deadly since the inability to present a clear and concise case to the proper *keeper* in turn results in more and more delays as one is passed on from *keeper* to *keeper*. In the long run despair, anguish, and inertia take their toll and little is accomplished. The final result is that the status quo remains in place.

The Bureaucracy

The *Great Hall of Paper* with its many *forms* lies within the university's larger bureaucratic system often known as the *"Labyrinth."* This is where the day to day operations of the university take place and where the *keepers* and all the other bureaucrats operate.

The *Labyrinth* is the muck and mire which pulls at one's heels and threatens to engulf those who dare to try to negotiate it. It is the process that slows one down and causes one to question why one even wants to go on. It quickly makes one realize and understand how inferior one is and how insignificant and powerless one can be when forced to deal with the system.

The single most evident truth in all bureaucracies is the reality that there really is no clear path by which one can navigate through the *Labyrinth*. It is a maze with many dead ends. While there may be formal systems in place, these do not guarantee success. In fact, the path to such success often lies through informal networking ties or by back door avenues.

Beating the System: Policies and Procedures

The linchpins to successfully dealing with the *Great Hall of Paper* and the *Labyrinth* lie in understanding university policy and procedure. If one can master the intricacies and nuisances of both then one gains the upper hand. It is therefore crucial that in order to be successful within these realms, an individual must become the resident expert on both.

To do so one must understand and quote the rules better than the ruler makers, one must know how to negotiate the back alleys of the bureaucracy better than the bureaucrats, and most importantly, one must know how to effectively identify and work with the right people.

Only when these skills are mastered can goals be accomplished and only then will one learn how to make the *Great Hall of Paper* and the *Labyrinth*, along with its minions the *keepers, and their* forms, work to one's advantage.

CHAPTER SIX

A CLOSER LOOK AT THE TRUTH BEHIND THE HIRING PROCESS: HOW UNIVERSITIES REALLY HIRE

Each year thousands of new faculty and staff members are hired to meet the growing demands of universities nationwide. During this process countless numbers of committees are formed to meet in what seems like endless hours of labor to screen candidates, evaluate credentials, and formulate plans to appoint the brightest and the best qualified to important positions within the schools.

Or so in theory it goes.

In reality though the hiring process is not based on a true meritocracy. The best qualified candidate in fact is not always the one who is offered the position. What occurs instead is a delicate balancing of several factors that result in a process that favors some candidates, is biased against others, but in the end provides a viable method for candidacy selection that works to perpetuate and reinforce the culture of a university and the beliefs of those who work there.

The Predispositions

As committees are formed and charged with their duties it is apparent from the outset that there are certain prevalent preferences regarding who should and should not be hired. One major predilection centers on the question of whether to hire from within the school or to seek candidates from outside the institution.

Hiring From Within A University

Hiring from within can be more cost effective if the university establishes the new pay rate for the internal candidate based upon the candidate's existing salary, as opposed to tying the salary rate to the position itself. When this occurs the internal candidate's salary, even with the pay increase, will often be far less than the initial starting salary of an outside hire.

A second benefit of hiring internal candidates is the fact that less time will be needed for overall training since the individuals are already familiar with the general practices and policies of the institution. More time can then be spent on helping them acquire the specific jobs skills necessary to be successful in their new positions.

The loyalty factor is also a major consideration when considering hiring an internal candidate. Individuals who are hired from within are more likely to be loyal to the institution. There is also a greater likelihood that the person will remain employed longer at the school, thus minimizing costly personnel turnovers. The longer individuals stay at the university, the more they are locked into the system, and the less likely they will be to contemplate making a career change to other institutions.

Finally, as individuals move up the hierarchy the greater their personal stake becomes in the university. A negative side of this "rise through the ranks" phenomenon is the fact that these individuals, not wishing to lose all that they have accomplished, begin to develop a real fear of making a mistake and possibly losing their jobs. This fear works to make them more supportive of the institution's positions and less likely to mount any serious opposition efforts. This in the long run though can stifle good ideas that are often born from discussion and dissent.

Hiring From Outside The University

On the other hand, hiring from outside the university has several unique advantages as well. Since individuals coming from other institutions are not familiar with the daily workings of the system it allows them to take a more critical look at its operations. From these observations improvements can be formulated. Often those who are mired in the daily bureaucratic routine do not see the value in changing it. Learning a new way to conduct business can be seen as unsettling; however change is essential for systematic improvements.

Loyalty also plays a key role when hiring from outside the school. In this case the loyalty is to the hiring administration and their policies, not the institution itself. In most cases the individuals will not question existing policies because of this loyalty factor. Executive power is thus reinforced as a result.

Very often universities decide to hire from outside their schools in order to make important policy or curriculum changes. Strong individuals who are hired from the outside can be used as the point people to implement new and possibly controversial policy changes. This is where the personal loyalty of the new hires pays benefits for the administration. In its most radical form these new individuals can even be charged with making extensive changes university-wide. In this scenario the people are brought in to "clean house." While doing so they will take the brunt of the criticism and work to insulate, in large part, the executive administration. In turn, for accomplishing these changes, the hires are given the opportunity to use their new found power and quickly establish their role in the school.

Finally, there is the reality that individuals hired from outside the school can bring with them a wealth of experience and can provide new and exciting ideas that would benefit the institution.

The decision to pursue internal or external candidates is an important one. It lays the foundation for the path the university will follow in the future.

The Impact of Hiring Committees

Hiring committees are designed to be objective. They are comprised of individuals who possess unique expertise within their fields. The ultimate goal for these individuals and their committees is to hire the most qualified individuals to fill the important vacant roles within the school. In theory, by utilizing their expertise and working through an equitable process the end result should be hiring recommendations from the committee, based upon objective criteria that eventually lead to the hiring of the best qualified candidates.

The reality though is that in many cases this is not what actually happens. Objectivity is often replaced by pure subjectivity and personal preference or bias. Committee members who foster strong personal opinions regarding candidates can unduly sway other members of the committee in favor of, or against, a candidate. Important senior members of the university faculty or staff can exert their power and hand pick or totally exclude candidates.

The formation of the committee can in many cases predetermine who will eventually be selected. Friends can be rewarded or vengeance can be brought down upon enemies. Knowing this, administrators are quick to select committee members who will best serve the needs of their departments.

As the process unfolds important committee discussions are conducted in complete secrecy. The committee is able to do so because accountability is minimal. What really occurs within these closed door sessions, including the manipulation and lobbying, is rarely recorded in the minutes of the meetings. As a result, the outcomes can be devastating, not only to the candidates, but to the school as well.

The Influencers

Powerful Individuals

Closely related to committee member selection is the fact that key powerful individuals at a university can greatly influence who will be hired. Top administrators, for example, can use their influence to advance the careers of their friends and colleagues. When this occurs qualifications become secondary. The result is that individuals are placed into administrative, faculty, or important staff positions with no real experience or expertise.

Powerful Groups

Administrators and individuals are not the only ones who can exert unwanted influence on the hiring process. In universities where powerful unions, faculty senates, or bargaining units exist, the hiring process can be unduly and unfairly influenced by the goals of these groups over the needs of the university.

The President

Finally, there is the use of the "Emperor's Clause." Presidents exert incredible power on most university campuses. The power of the president is second only to the power of the Board of Trustees. In most cases it is unchallenged. Presidents have the final say in almost all matters regarding the actual day to day running of the university. As such, presidents can accept the recommendations brought forth by the hiring committee, ignore any and all submissions and select whichever candidate they deem best, or bypass the entire hiring process and simply outright appoint candidates to positions on an interim or permanent basis.

Most presidents are very careful to allow the hiring process to play out, however, in key positions the ultimate selection of the candidate comes down to the president's wishes. The leadership style of the president will determine who is ultimately hired and who will be in power to make important daily decisions at the university. If the president values innovative and creative approaches to solving problems, or believes in open debate that leads to informed decision making, then candidates that challenge the president's ideas will be hired. If on the other hand the president prefers to wield total power and to only implement ideas that spring from the president's office, like Athena from Zeus or Chrysaor from Medusa, then a cadre of "yes" individuals will emerge from the ranks of the candidates.

The interplay between and among any or all of these influential individuals and groups significantly impacts on who is hired on a university campus.

The Minority Factor

"This University is an equal opportunity and affirmative action institution that does not discriminate in its hiring process with regard to color, sex, age, religion, sexual orientation, national origin, race, political affiliation, marital status, veteran status, or physical or mental disability. Women, minorities, and the physically challenged are encouraged to apply."

Variations of this statement accompany every university job advertisement. It sounds fair. It appears as though any qualified individual would have an equal opportunity to apply and win a position within the university.

The reality is that the minority factor weighs heavily in final hiring decisions.

If a university decides that different perspectives are not essential or valuable, if it decides that the richness that diversity brings to a campus is not as important as maintaining the status quo, then no matter how qualified an individual who applies for a position may be, the possibility of that person receiving a fair opportunity to secure employment is remote.

On the other hand, if a university believes that meeting minority goals is the paramount criterion for hiring, even if more qualified candidates exist, then the result will be an imbalance favoring specific groups. If this occurs, then in the final analysis, hiring the best qualified candidate will yield to hiring only the best qualified minority and the belief in equal opportunity will become a myth.

Building upon the logic expressed in Aristotle's <u>Nicomachean Et</u>, the maxim "too little or too much of anything is not a good thing" directly applies here. Under or over representation of any group results in a negative impact in all areas of the university from policy making decisions to classroom instruction.

Universities struggle each day to find a workable balance between making sure that diverse groups are represented on campus and at the same time ensuring that qualified individuals are hired.

<u>Miscellaneous Factors</u>

Other important factors, some of which may be beyond a university's control, can impact considerably on the hiring process.

Salary

Salary is often a key determinant in hiring. Very often the best candidate will decline an offer to join the university because of the compensation that is offered. This is particularly true when the cost of living within a community far exceeds the starting salary range. It is not unusual for a candidate to refuse a job offer after coming to the realization that the average price of housing within the school's geographical area is ten to fifteen times higher than the beginning salary.

Not The First Choice

Another predominant factor that weights heavily on hiring is the reality that very often universities are forced to settle for a committee's third or even fourth choice because the leading candidates have refused an offer to work within their schools. The result is that the individuals who are finally hired are acceptable, but not the best choices.

It's Still Who You Know, And Who Knows You, That Counts

Certain intangible factors also play a role in the hiring process. For example, at times candidates will be given preference because they have relatives or close friends working at the institution. It might not always be outright nepotism however, a little extra consideration, including being granted an interview, can go a long way.

The Results

Good hiring must be firmly grounded in the implementation of an equitable hiring policy based upon merit. If instead, influence, power, or inequitable policy guidelines are the main determinants in who is hired, then the impact on a university will be disastrous.

Shared Governance

Input from all segments of the university community are essential if the best candidates are to be hired. If this does not occur and crucial decision making is left to powerful individuals or groups alone, then the results will be the creation of a powerful pro forma dictatorship or a small power centered oligarchy controlled by individuals who can make unilateral uncontested decisions.

Effects

There are significant short and long term deleterious effects of an unfair or biased hiring process.

Short Term Effects

In the short term, if candidates are hired that endorse the old "business as usual" policies of the university, the result will be less thinking "outside the box." Innovative thinking and creativity will suffer and individuals will see little value in taking risks. Innovation, creativity, and risk taking are crucial elements in the growth of any university.

Long Term Effects

One long term consequence of an unfair hiring process will be the effect it will have on the employees of the university. The impact on employees will become quite evident. They will experience little personal satisfaction and fulfillment. Faculty and staff will become "drone-like." They will just go through the motions and conduct "business as usual." In turn, they will also feel little need to make a lasting commitment to the school. Eventually, employees mired in this situation will be faced with the choices of leaving the school, denying reality, or experiencing cognitive dissonance.

The biggest impact of all will be felt on the university system itself. It will eventually breakdown. The university's vision will become blurred and institutional goals will go unfilled. Resources will be depleted and valuable time will be wasted on endless and fruitless searches.

Conclusions

It is evident that a perfect hiring system does not exist. There will always be those who inappropriately exert their influence and power. The stark reality is that the best qualified candidate will not always be hired.

It is paramount though that universities provide as fair a hiring process as is humanly possible. Without it tragically, and most regrettably, students will suffer and their needs will go unmet.

The logic is simple and sound. Good people make good schools and good schools help develop good students. If the avenues for hiring good people are blocked, then the future of the institution and all that it is dedicated to accomplishing will be threatened.

CHAPTER SEVEN

PORTRAIT OF THE UNIVERSITY EMPLOYEE: WORK 'EM TO DEATH, OR JUST LEAVE 'EM ALONE.

Everyday in hundreds of institutions of higher education throughout the nation thousands of employees report to work and go about their business of completing their assigned duties in small eight hour blocks of time.

Within this group of workers exists two distinct groups of individuals who possess unique qualities that make them stand out from each other. Each practice a special type of work ethic philosophy that helps define it as employees and as people.

<u>"Sure, I'll do it."</u>

The first group is comprised of those workers that not only show up to work on time every day and work diligently to complete their job tasks, but who also come to work early and stay late. These are the workers that the university comes to rely upon. They are the work horses of the university system. These are the faceless individuals who keep the system humming along smoothly.

Although they lack any special talent, these are the individuals who volunteer for committee work and special project assignments. They are the people who "help out" in almost every cause without being asked. They are the "go to" people. They are often anonymous and work behind the scenes and have learned to blend in. They are almost never well paid, and yet, they are the ones a university can always count on.

What makes these individuals so dedicated? What makes them so willing to do so much for so little?

There are several answers to these questions. One lies within the personalities of the individuals themselves. There exists in certain individuals a real desire to prove their worth. These individuals are self motivated. Often they are people oriented. They seek to please others by working hard and they take pride in their efforts. In some cases they are even perfectionists who demand extremely high or even impossible levels of excellence in themselves. They are driven to achieve this excellence and perfection. These individuals are also exceptional team players who place the importance of the school and the work they do, over any individual success or acknowledgement. When working with others who may not share such beliefs of perfection and excellence, they assume the added responsibility of "picking up the slack" and doing more than their share to ensure success. When projects are completed they are often too humble to take credit for their extra efforts or any success that resulted from their hard work. They prefer to share the credit equally with colleagues even if they shouldered most of the work burden.

It soon becomes apparent to everyone that these individuals are willing to do whatever needs to be done to ensure that the targeted goals are met. Others sometimes take advantage of this fact and these individuals are abused by colleagues who are more than willing to allow them to shoulder the burden and sacrifice their time in order to complete the work. In the process, their welfare soon becomes secondary to the needs of the institution and other individuals.

Yet, it seems that no matter how much extra work is asked of them, they find a way to do it. They complete whatever must get done on time and usually do an excellent job in doing so. Interestingly enough, they rarely raise their voices in protest to complain. Seldom, if ever, are these individuals afforded the recognition they deserve.

<u>"No way, not me."</u>

In the very same workforce though there exists another and quite different type of employee. In sharp contrast to the ever present and hard working group of individuals, there also exist those employees who have mastered the ability to do very little and yet survive, and even at times to thrive, within the university system.

In a system that it not merit based, and does not directly reward effort with financial and professional success, these types of individuals have learned that a strong work ethic does not guarantee recognition, nor does effort always lead to commensurate rewards. They learn very quickly that except in rare cases, just about "everyone" gets the same pay raises, that just about "everyone" moves along in their career paths at the same pace, and that seniority is often far more important than hard work.

If it is true that the system gives everyone, no matter how much effort was expended, basically the same rewards for their efforts, than it stands to reason that workers who only fulfill minimum acceptable standards of responsibility come to realize that they are just as likely to achieve as much career success as those who work far more diligently than they do.

These individuals come to realize that it makes far more sense not to take risks because risks can lead to mistakes. Mistakes get individuals noticed quickly and mistakes are punished far more severely than lack of effort. One significant mistake can even result in dismissal, and yet seldom will plain laziness lead to loss of employment. It is simply easier, and far less risky, to just do one's job, and nothing more. These individuals quickly learn that by only doing what is required of them, they will seldom get into trouble. Unfortunately, risk taking is vital for needed changes in any organization. When individuals refuse to take risks or try new ideas the university becomes stagnant and there is little or no growth.

One of the interesting side effects of this conscious decision on the part of these individuals to not exert any extra effort, or not to volunteer to do more than what is expected of them, is the realization by others within the university that these people should not be counted upon to "go the extra mile." They should not be relied upon to complete any additional assigned work on time, nor to do an exceptional job under any circumstances. These people come to be known as those who are most likely to say "no" when approached to help out, the people who are the "naysayers" who believe that nothing is worth the effort, and the people who are "unenthusiastic" about everything. Since these individuals exhibit such beliefs, they are eventually excluded from any new initiatives and are never approached to do any additional work. Instead others are asked to step up and do even more when it is needed. The result is that the overworked become even more overburdened.

And on and on it goes

Somehow in spite of these obvious and blatant inequalities the university system continues to hum along as these two diametrically opposed set of individuals continue to work in an unspoken harmony. The "worker bees" quietly keep giving more than 100% while their unmotivated and apathetic colleagues continue to collect their monthly paychecks and simply "mark time" on their way toward retirement. As long as the work somehow gets done no one makes a concerted effort to change the system. Everyone just leaves it well enough alone.

The result is that the vast majority of employees robotically march along to eerie similar daily routines while some individuals are greatly overworked and others simply refuse to make any type of commitment or accept any real responsibility. Individuals soon learn to echo the beliefs that "only suckers volunteer" for extra work and that "the only reward for good work, is more work."

Strategies for necessary change

It is imperative that universities develop strategies to avoid these inequities and in the process somehow find a way to re-motivate those who simply do their jobs, but no more. These may include the establishment of an annual merit or bonus system to financially reward those individuals who have exceeded their goals during the year; the development of a well defined process to promote outstanding individuals; a closer and more detailed analysis of existing job descriptions in order to make needed changes in individual and departmental responsibilities; or even a systematic analysis of how the workload is distributed throughout the work place in order to ensure that all employees are asked to contribute to the needs of the institution equally.

These and other needed changes will in the end force all individuals, and the institutions themselves, to become accountable for their actions. This accountability will guarantee that a university's visions and goals are reinforced and that the needs of all students are met. Without this accountability institutional foundational beliefs will quietly erode away unnoticed.

CHAPTER EIGHT

THE COMMITTEE:
THE MIDWIFE FOR NEW IDEAS

Committee!

The dreaded nine letter word that spreads loathing and frustration throughout the academic community.

Those within the university setting know the word all too well. Even though most universities require their personnel to serve on at least one or two annually, many individuals spend a good deal of their time avoiding participation on them.

Both within and outside of academia the perception of committee work is usually quite negative. Fred Allen called a committee "A group...

who individually can do nothing but as a group decide that nothing can be done" (Best Quotes, 2011).

This belief that committees hinder and forestall needed change is quite prevalent within many universities. As a result, often committees are seen as ineffective and its members' efforts viewed as a waste of valuable time.

The reality is though, that whether or not they are seen as inefficient, they are indeed crucial to higher education. They are in fact the lifeblood of a university.

No matter the size of the school, no matter its mission or focus, no matter the breath of its resources, committees are an integral institutionalized part of the day to day running of any institution.

Throughout a university there are many different types of committees designed to fulfill specific functions within well-defined areas of influence.

The University Level

Committee work on the university level is seen as critical to a school's mission.

There are many committees formed on this level to meet specific needs. Some are more important than others. One of the most important university committees is the Strategic Planning Committee. This group helps develop a university's vision as well as formulate strategies to plan and guide the institution's future.

There are also varied leadership committees on the university level that work to teach effective leadership skills to present and future leaders at the school.

Other important university committees include budget committees, tenure granting committees, and curriculum committees, to name but a few.

Each and every one of these committees is tasked with dealing with issues that affect the institution as a whole.

The Department Level

On the department level there is also a wide array of committees. Some of these are faculty based including faculty hiring committees, tenure recommendation committees, and handbook committees. Others such as department curriculum committees deal with the development, revision, and implementation of new courses or programs. There can be accreditation or assessment committees on the departmental level as well. There can even be committees designed to self police department policies and personnel.

The Student Level

Universities establish key student centered committees. These include committees dealing with admission and enrollment standards. There are committees to hear student appeals about grades, or readmission, or even faculty complaints. There are also committees to monitor the progress of students, and still others to set academic and disciplinary policies and procedures.

All are viewed as vital for providing a quality education to the students.

The Committee Structure

Committees can be standing committees with fixed responsibilities or temporary ad hoc committees, including taskforces established to accomplishing specific goals. These temporary committees include such entities as steering committees for accreditation, budget committees, crisis committees, building committees, fundraising committees, and even flu committees.

Within the organizational bureaucratic structure of the committee framework committees are often divided into sub-committees. These smaller versions of the larger committee are assigned specific goals to achieve. The belief is that people working on specific tasks will function more efficiently. These sub-committees also in theory work to promote shared governance by involving a larger number of faculty and staff, who in turn provide more input and greater "buy in" to the goals of the committee.

In the day to day operations of a university there can be literally dozens and dozens of committees all working simultaneously and supposedly in coordination with each other. Together they greatly impact the daily work and lives of faculty, staff, and students.

Ineffective Committees

Charles Kettering said that "If you want to kill any idea in the world today, get a committee working on it" (Best Quotes, 2011).

It is true that some committees are inefficient and some actually hinder more than help the overall goals of a university. In fact, at times some committees make a concerted effort to derail any new initiatives. This can be done for several reasons. Committees may simply decide to maintain the status quo out of fear of causing problems. In conjunction with this is the belief that no one can get into trouble if nothing is done. At other times the thought is that if no initiatives are moved forward, than no extra work and no new resources would be required. When any of these occur important opportunities to make valuable changes are thwarted.

It is also true that there is no guarantee that a committee's decision will be correct or in the best interest of a university or its students. David Coblit points out "A committee can make a decision that is dumber than any of its members" (Best Quotes, 2011).

Although committee participation can be a time consuming inefficient process which can often be frustrating and produce questionable results, for the most part the use of committees is preferable to the alternative. This would be a top down decision making model with very little input from departments, faculty, staff, or students.

New Initiatives

Committees, if utilized effectively, can be successful avenues for planting seeds for important ideas. For example, if an individual wishes to champion a special initiative or bring an important idea to the forefront, that person can begin by introducing the idea at a committee meeting. If that individual then serves on a second committee the idea can then be reintroduced at that committee's meeting as well with the additional benefit of being able to state that the idea had been already discussed at a previous meeting.

It is not necessary to divulge the fact that it was the individual who presented the idea initially. It is sufficient to state that the idea was discussed elsewhere.

The key here is for an individual to be on as many committees as possible so the process can be repeated over and over again gaining more momentum each time. Eventually, as this momentum grows the individual will be able to reintroduce the idea in committee after committee and report that the initiative is being discussed on a wide scale in multiple committees.

Consequently, as the idea is discussed in a number of committees in this manner there is less and less incentive for someone to challenge the idea since "it is being discussed all across campus." Effectively employing this strategy also gives an individual the opportunity to piggyback one idea on another.

Personal Incentives

The key for any individual working within a university is to select the proper committees on which to serve. Careful selection and participation in the more important and influential committees will not only provide opportunities to develop and implement key needed initiatives, it will also enhance one's own personal sphere of influence in the process.

Committee participation can be advantageous for the individual in several other ways.

Actively serving and especially chairing a committee, makes the individual seem dedicated to a university and its causes. These committees also work to build personal power bases by allowing the individual greater input into the decision making process and by providing the opportunity to network with key university personnel.

Committee participation also provides those who work on them the opportunity to gain inside knowledge and information not available to those who do not serve. This knowledge allows committee members to have a better understanding of what is occurring on campus and to see the "bigger picture" regarding campus strategies, allocation of resources, initiatives, and even campus politics. They are privy to both current and future university plans and goals. This information can prove invaluable on many levels.

Conclusions

In the final analysis most committees are effective and are beneficial to the smooth and efficient running of a university. As such, they are worthwhile and will continue to be an integral part of the operation of any campus.

More importantly, committees will also continue to serve as the venue for academic change within a university. Therefore it just makes good sense for an individual to serve on as many committees as time and energy will allow. This service will most assuredly result in both professional and personal gain for any individual who is willing to put in the extra time and effort.

If individuals understand the real importance of committee work they may be able to see that this nine letter word called "committee" can lead to another more sought after nine letter word, "promotion;" promotion of an individual's ideas; promotion of an individual's professional success; and promotion of an individual's personal influence and power.

As Graham Summer so rationally advocated "If you live in a country run by committee, be on the committee" (Best Quotes, 2011).

This advice is well worth heeding.

CHAPTER NINE

WORKING THE UNIVERSITY SYSTEM: STRATEGIES FOR BUILDING A PERSONAL POWERBASE

How does an individual build a strong powerbase within a university community? Power is important. From power comes the ability to create and implement new ideas and initiatives. From power comes the opportunity to develop policy and control practice. From power comes personal and career benefits.

Within each university system there are prescribed formalized methods for accomplishing tasks and achieving established goals. To truly understand how a university, or any large organization functions, it is vital to understand the basis of the formal structure. Those individuals who understand formal systems within a university can use this knowledge to their advantage. By observing and applying what they have learned they can in turn then work within the system to achieve their own personal goals.

Know Who To Back

Personal networking within the formal hierarchy can provide extraordinary avenues for championing ideas. There is a defined "ranked based" pecking order within any university. There are those at the very top and those at the very bottom. There are however a myriad of layers in the middle ranks filled with individuals who hold equivalent rank and wield almost equal power. Within this power vacuum individuals employ a variety of strategies in order to implement their ideas. Some are more successful than others and at times it can become a "my guy" versus "your guy" situation with the outcome very often in doubt. The key is to know how to select a side wisely and at what point to back the right individual. Caution is the key word here. Be patient and weigh all options before committing. In the best case scenario it is even possible to effectively stay on the "winning side" without seeming to take sides at all.

This strategy can be of major advantage for individuals. Through these contacts important initiatives can be implemented, while at the same time personal networking bonds can be developed.

Staying "In The Know"

Built into the university system are internal structures to ensure that the formal system is functional and effective. The system, for example, is comprised of a defined hierarchy with a well delineated chain of command. As stated, this hierarchy is designed to be "position and rank based" with the most powerful people at the top controlling key decisions. Since this is the case, keeping those in these powerful positions in the information loop is essential. Through this information these bosses will make decisions that will impact upon their departments, divisions, and the university itself. As such these individuals do not like surprises. They do not like being caught off guard at a meeting when they discover that others possess information that they should have known as well. Conversely, careers can be greatly benefited by providing the boss with important information in a timely manner. It is essential therefore to keep these individuals informed.

The key though is to determine when to share vital information and with whom to share it. Passing along vital information without gaining any personal benefit only serves to bolster others' influence and power. This delicate balancing act of knowing which information to share and when to share it is crucial for developing power within a university.

Use The Chain of Command

In addition to providing a steady stream of information to those above, it is also important to remember that when issues arise, it is key to work through the chain of command, even if the problem is an immediate supervisor. Those in power routinely chant the mantra that that they are "approachable" and "open minded" even if they are in reality closed minded micro-managers. It is important to be open and upfront about any issues that may arise. If individuals choose to work secretively, unless they are extremely clever, they are unknowingly setting a trap for themselves by providing an opportunity for their supervisors to use this secrecy against them. People and organizations do not respect individuals who work behind others' backs. This is especially true for supervisors. The old maxim that "it is better to go through the boss than around the boss" is true. By doing so individuals are viewed as open, honest, and people of integrity. Utilizing the chain of command then works to their benefit.

Once again it is important to understand though that this drastic tactic of "going over someone's head" must be done only in the most extreme situations and when the result will work to the benefit of the individual performing this action. Careers are made and broken with such decisions.

Be The Rules "Expert"

In order for the formal system to function smoothly institutional policies are developed. These are usually well-defined and help establish the "rules" by which the organization runs on a daily basis. Here again though problems can arise. As the university grows, so too do the number of policies. The end result is that over time these policies become so numerous that for practical reasons no one truly understands all of them or knows which ones to use in all cases. Individuals become familiar with only those policies that directly pertain to their daily activities or areas of work. They seldom know, or understand, policies that are outside their sphere of influence.

Policies are often vague, redundant, and occasionally appear to be in direct contradiction to each other. This causes confusion at times on which policy to apply. Individuals can use this confusion to their advantage and benefit. As mentioned earlier, by knowing all the key policies and understanding when to apply each in specific circumstances, individuals will have the advantage of being able to use the policy that benefits them the most in situations where conflicting policies are at hand.

In addition, by knowing the policies these individuals eventually become the ones that others will turn to when confusion arises. Others soon learn that it is just easier to ask the "resident expert" which policy

Joseph S.C. Simplicio Ph.D.

applies, instead of trying to determine it themselves. As a result, these individuals become the "go to" people and their power grows.

Conclusions

While there are several other important career lessons to learn within a working environment, these strategies are rudimentary, but yet key components in building a successful career. From their foundations come opportunities to implement personal ideas and initiatives. Whether a first year employee or a seasoned veteran, it is essential to master these techniques in order to build a successful career and carve out a powerbase within a university.

CHAPTER TEN

KEY WAYS TO BUILD BASES OF INFLUENCE WITHIN A UNIVERSITY

<u>The American University</u>

In many ways universities occupy a unique niche within the American Society. Their success for example, is not measured in productivity or simply quantifiable numbers. In addition, while business practices apply to some extent, and financial matters are important, accountability is not measured solely and simply in terms of these factors.

In other ways though universities are very much like their corporate counterparts. There is a fixed hierarchy and there are established rules and procedures for conducting daily business. Within a university culture there are also existing avenues for acquiring personal power and influence.

There are strategies to develop that powerbase through interactions with others in the university community.

Develop Opportunities for Success

Just about everyone wants to be successful in what they do. This is true on the university campus as well. Many people fail because their talents are not effectively utilized for their benefit or the benefit of the institution. A good supervisor has the ability to find a person's strength, to discover what that person does well, and then play to that strength. This provides the person with opportunities to succeed and success is contagious and builds upon itself.

Ideas

In order to help others be successful it is important at times to give away good ideas. These help the individual buy into and take ownership of the idea. Individuals are more willing to commit time and resources to their own ideas. This strategy also helps them become more successful within a university. These individuals will in turn attribute their success in part to the person who gave them the idea.

The key here is to only give away "good" ideas, but never give away "great" ideas. Good ideas help a university, but great ideas are career changers.

No Losers

Dealing with individuals over issues can be stressful. At times people can even become confrontational. This confrontation often sets up a win/lose scenario where one person walks away as the victor and the other as the vanquished. First of all, people do not buy into ideas they do not believe in and they will not work effectively with people whom they believe do not share their beliefs. Silencing people in a discussion does not mean that they agree. It also does not guarantee that they will help implement other's ideas.

Secondly, the people that individuals work with today are probably the same people they will work with tomorrow. Individuals may be successful one day in getting their ideas across only to find that they are not as successful the next day on another issue. If a person is perceived as someone who "has to win" that person will find it very difficult to work with others when they do not wield the power. It is therefore critical to avoid such situations for many reasons. In the best case scenario everyone gets something and the idea moves forward.

Finally, it is also important to be extremely careful in one's selection of language. Try to use language that is as professional and as non-personal as possible. Avoid using words that other people will find offensive. Above all, never attack. People have long memories and harmful words or actions can damage future interactions.

It's Not Personal

An important credo to understand when dealing with colleagues is the reality that anything that is said to or about you will be viewed as not personal. It is assumed that you should be able to accept criticism without taking it personally. It is just business.

On the other hand, it is important to understand that anything that you say about others will in turn always be viewed as very personal. You will not be able to criticize the idea without criticizing the person who developed it. The lesson is to accept criticism graciously, even thankfully, but at the same time use criticism very sparingly. As far back as the sixth century B.C. Aesop was able to point out in his famous fable, The Man and the Serpent, that "Injuries may be forgiven, but never forgotten." If an individual is able to master this skill, that person will be very successful within a university.

Think of the Future

As stated, many of the people that individuals must deal with on specific occasions will be the same people, or friends of the same people, that they will be forced to interact with in future endeavors. As the dramatist Wilson Mizner observed, "Be nice to people on your way up because you'll meet them on your way down." (The Colombia World of Quotations, 1996). It is crucial therefore to only burn bridges strategically and as a last resort. Openly attacking another or the ideas that person represents should only be done in order to accomplish greater goals. In the sixteenth century Machiavelli said, "If an injury has to be done to a man it should be so severe that his vengeance need not be feared." (Bartlett's Familiar Quotations, 2007). This can usually only be done when a person is leaving, or has left the institution, or when that person is in no real position to seek revenge. An example of this would be a vote of no confidence against someone who has no power to retaliate.

Build a Base

A strong set of allegiances is crucial to any powerbase. In addition to a small cadre of close reliable friends the key to establishing such a base is to draw from all segments of a university community. Alliances should be formed with everyone from executive administration to those who work in facilities operations. Each area of a university, from the most powerful to those who toil in anonymity, offers the opportunity to work closely with people with different specialties, talents, and abilities to contribute. Those who hold positions of influence for example, can be helpful in pushing through important initiatives. Peers on the other hand afford the opportunity to create a close group of friends and colleagues that forge a sense of solidarity in cause and purpose. Even those who seemingly have little or no power can still provide needed support. Their numbers can be a deciding factor at crucial times.

Those Who Are Forgotten

It is essential to include those who provide services to a university. These include administrative staff, clerical help, security, and even the lunch room lady. Once befriended, each can be counted on to provide support when needed. These individuals also provide access to other people and access to resources. Access allows for freedom and a more effective use of the informal university system. In addition to building a strong support base and gaining access to resources, working with all of these individuals will help foster a "man of the people" persona.

Closely related to this though is the understanding that these alliances shift very quickly. As such, an individual must be ready to add or replace allies, firmly understanding that to rely on any one individual or group too much can be a fatal mistake.

Be Accessible

It is important that an individual be viewed as more than just approachable. In order to foster the idea that an individual is "there" for everyone it is essential that the individual be willing to go above and beyond the norm. That means making offers to help a colleague with everything from work related projects to personal problems. At times it may mean offering to loan money to a co-worker making it clear that there is no anticipation of repayment. Just making the offer is usually enough to "do the trick."

<u>Listen</u>

The most important aspect of being accessible is the willingness to sit and listen. Volumes have been written on the importance of listening. There are a myriad of strategies that tell how to be effective listeners. There is passive listening, active listening, contextual listening, conceptual listening, and many other techniques that make an individual a better listener. Listening is indeed important. It is not enough just to be accessible to people. It is essential that a person be available to listen to what is being said. This means always being ready to listen to a colleague who needs to be heard. It means stopping what is being done and giving that person full attention. It means not answering the telephone, not continuing to work while someone is talking, and not allowing any interruptions or distractions to break the flow of the conversation.

Listening means fighting the urge and temptation to try to solve that problem or give examples from one's experiences about what has been done or could be done. It also means being non-judgmental. Most importantly, listening is just that, it is remaining silent and taking in what is being said. It is crucial to remember that this is not about anyone but the person. In most cases this person simply wants someone to talk to, not someone to solve the problem.

When this is done, it tells the person that it is understood that what is being said is important. More importantly, it says that one is never too busy to listen. Making time for people communicates the message that they are important. While this may seem difficult at times, imagine if someone were to offer a colleague $1,000, but insisted on counting it out one dollar a time. Most people would find the time to allow that person to do so. So must time be found to listen to colleagues.

While listening it is important that the individual shows a genuine interest in what is being said. Body language is key here. Lean forward and concentrate on what the person is saying. A subtle nodding of the head is also effective and reassuring. It lets the person know that someone is listening.

If others believe that they have a good shoulder on which to cry, and a good friend who will listen, they will be more likely to form a closer bond with that individual. Networking and powerbases grow from such bonding.

Know When To Get Even

The harsh reality of life is that not everyone is nice. Some people are not willing to work in a "give and take" society for mutual benefit. Some people are greedy and calculating. These are the people everyone loath. Situations make it impossible to be nice to everyone, and it is a mistake to treat these individuals with respect and kindness. It shows weakness to try to do so. These individuals must be dealt with, and at times dealt with ruthlessly.

Understanding that it is not possible to bring these types of individuals into the fold it is important at times to actively work for their demise within the institution. To "bring down" such people shows an individual's power. Such actions also work as deterrents for others who might wish to be confrontational.

Conclusions

Effectively interacting with the individuals who collectively comprise a university community can work to build personal power and influence. It is important to understand that what is important to others can in turn build support for what is important to one's own ideas.

CHAPTER ELEVEN

THE PERSONAL TOUCH

There are two main avenues for acquiring power. The first is rooted in the job position. Being the boss means people have to listen to what you say, or pay the consequences. Unfortunately, becoming the boss can take years of hard work. There is also no guarantee that such hard work will be rewarded with promotions and career advancements. In addition, bosses are often disliked and others sometimes actively work to undermine a boss' authority. In the end, bosses come and go and personal power that is position based is fleeting.

In tandem with this formal system there also co-exists an informal system for getting things done. At times these two systems work in unison, at other times they mirror or complement each other as employees go about the daily working of the school. At other times though they come into direct conflict.

Through this informal system exists a second avenue to power which relies on the use of personal and institutional networking to achieve goals. This strategy may not result in ultimate power, but it produces a powerbase that is more enduring and often broader based. Unlike power that stems from a specific job or title, this power allows the individual to avoid the major pitfalls that power can bring. With this form of power there is little, if any, open rivalry or resentment from colleagues. There is also a closeness that develops that provides access to information, and with that information the opportunity to build more networking and an even stronger powerbase.

It is important to understand how the informal network of personal ties allows the institution, and the people who work there, to survive and grow. Those individuals who understand the informal systems within a university can use this knowledge to their advantage.

The Informal System

Is it possible to use the system for one's own personal gain? The answer is a resounding yes. To do so one must understand the informal structures that make up the fabric of a university community. It also means being willing to utilize cold hard tactics for developing alliances and bases of influences. The approaches at times may seem Machiavellian at heart, but the real focus is to allow for the opportunity for individuals to incorporate the traits of Socrates' Philosopher King as described in Plato's <u>Republic</u> as well.

<u>Alliances Form When The Formal System Breaks Down</u>

In theory, several key factors are put in place to ensure that the formal system is functional and effective. One of these key factors is based upon the fact, as previously mentioned, that the formal system within a university is comprised of a defined hierarchy with a well delineated chain of command. In theory, employees utilized this top to bottom down system to discuss issues, solve problems, develop ideas, and carry out policies. The hierarchy is designed to be position based with the most qualified people rising to the top. As such, it is therefore designed to be objective with decisions being made based upon what is good for the university.

In reality, the system is not truly objective and the people who are the policy makers are not always the most qualified and they very often use their power subjectively. The result is that it benefits some individuals while placing others at a disadvantage. The bottom line is that in many cases it is still "who you know, and who knows you" that matters and personal alliances are still the most effective avenue for accomplishing both institutional and personal goals. Clever people within the organization understand which individuals make up the most important alliances and how to use these alliances for their own personal benefit.

Make the Extra Effort

Smile and Show Those Pearly Whites

The number one strategy for acquiring power that leads to personal gain within the university system is to develop a friendly and outgoing personality. People like to help other people who are nice. The grump does not garnish favor with many individuals. On the other hand, the sweet, outgoing, humorous, and friendly person is welcomed. A smiling face is a passport to friendship. Once the chance to establish a friendship is offered it is important to build on this opportunity. This can be accomplished in several ways.

The Compliment

One of the most successful strategies for building friendships and in turn spheres of influence is the effective and timely use of the compliment. Individuals like to hear that they are doing a good job, and more importantly that they are good people. Through the use of compliments an individual is able to not only make people feel good and show that they are important, they are able in turn to develop a special rapport that can be used in the future. It is essential though that these compliments be genuine. Individuals will eventually see though disingenuous and pandering remarks.

<u>Visits Help Develop Personal Contacts</u>

The importance of personal contacts is crucial to the establishment of networking ties that will work to the benefit of the individual. In order to establish these networks it is important to take time each day to stop and speak with colleagues. Extended visits, or simply stopping in to say a quick hello will pay big dividends. While there, make sure to look around at pictures on the desk or diplomas on the wall. Ask questions about family, hobbies, career ambitions, and anything else that the individual wishes to discuss. Get to know the names of their children. People like other people who take an interest in their lives and what is important to them. The Great Napoleon inspired his troops to fight to the death for him because he took the time to learn the names of his soldiers' wives and children. He established a personal connection with his troops and they responded with total loyalty to him as both a leader and a man.

During these discussions look for common areas of agreement. Finding these common areas help others to see that there are mutually shared interests and that the visitor is very much like them. It also gives the impression that they can most likely expect support when needed. It is during these sessions that individuals can create connections that will help with future needs.

Another variation on this strategy is to send congratulatory and thank you notes for everything from a job well done to a birthday wish.

Just because individuals do things that are part of their jobs does not mean that they should not be thanked for doing them. People remember others who remember them.

Informal Lines of Communication

Closely related to creating personal ties is the need to develop a working knowledge of who to talk to and when to talk to them when issues arise. Many a problem has been short circuited by speaking to the right person at the right time. The right person can be anyone from an administrative assistant all the way up to the president. This person is the one that has the ability to initiate a course of action to achieve the desired result. It is evident that these people will be more inclined to do so if they are part of an individual's networking system. Again, personal ties are crucial in establishing these connections. Individuals are more likely to help others with whom they have personal ties rather than because the individual asking for the help has more power. In fact, those in a subordinate position often see it as a good opportunity when they are able to help a superior. They see it as banking a favor for a future date.

Humility

Humility is viewed as a very positive attribute. People want their leaders to not only be brilliant and powerful, but humble at the same time. Individuals who forget this lesson soon lose their influence and eventually their power. As the Bible states in Proverbs 16:18, "Pride goes before destruction and haughtiness before a fall." However, as Proverbs 29:23 points out, "Humility brings honor." At times this means even making fun or denigrating oneself. People who can laugh at themselves are seen as good, honest, and down to earth people who are not too serious and know how to have fun.

Humor

Closely related to the idea of humility is the real need for a sense of humor. The workday can be long and arduous. It is important to break up the routine and doldrums with a little laughter. People like to be around humorous people. There is a subtle difference though between being the office clown and the person who knows how to make people laugh. Simply telling jokes or acting silly are not sound strategies for employing humor in the workplace effectively. Humor should be spontaneous. It should be born out of the moment and based upon the situation. Timing is key, as is knowing how far to go. This kind of humor is viewed as witty and the person making the comments is often seen as intelligent and even a little bit rebellious. Whether making a pithy comment about the university or utilizing just the right touch of sarcasm to make a point, this person is seen as a little bit courageous and someone who is willing to express what others are often thinking, but are afraid to say out loud.

Stay Hungry

The final piece of advice for those who wish to use the university's informal structure system effectively for their own personal success is to remember that, "those who do not remain hungry eventually get eaten." It is imperative that an individual remain active, establishing new contacts, developing new bonds of loyalty, and the hundred other daily activities that will guarantee that this individual will remain influential within the university. To do otherwise is not only a major mistake, but a formula for personal, social, and academic suicide.

CHAPTER TWELVE

THE ART OF THE FAVOR: THE CONNECTION BETWEEN NETWORKING AND PERSONAL INFLUENCE WITHIN A UNIVERSITY

Favors

Building favors is essential to creating a network of individuals that can be counted on for favors in turn. Favors translate into future obligations. There are several ways to build these favors. Primary among these include the strategic use of budgetary funds and the empowering of people and their ideas.

Budget

The effective use of a budget is one of the most important ways to grant favors. When individuals control the budget, they are in position to control resources that can provide key individuals with what they need and want. These can range from small practical everyday office or personal items to larger program building equipment. The budget can provide both the practical and the grand. The key is knowing when, to whom, and where to distribute the funds.

Empower Others

Successfully building favors also rests on the idea of learning how to empower co-workers and colleagues. This is best accomplished by establishing the reputation of being an individual who believes in others' ideas. As such an individual it is important to work to try to bring these ideas to reality. Attempts to do so can be through either the formal bureaucratic system or through networking with other individuals.

Advocating for others and their ideas means being willing to speak up on their behalf. Attitude is crucial here. It is good to be seen as the person who is willing to take risks and one who is willing to move forward the new ideas of others. The difference between saying, "let's see if we can find a way to make this happen, if not now then sometime down the road for sure" or saying "I don't know if this will work" is immeasurable. Being seen as the "can do" person is a major asset. Even if the answer is eventually no, the effort will still be perceived as noble.

Speaking on the behalf of others also means that at certain times an individual must be willing to fight for the "underdog." This can prove to be very beneficial to one's career. Backing the long shot instantly bestows on the individual the mark of a champion of the people.

Sometimes a cause manifests itself in the fight for "the principle" instead of for a specific individual. Others are quick to praise colleagues who are willing to fight for the ideal. They understand that the principle is worth preserving because they may need it one day for their own cause.

Believing in the ideas of others or fighting for the greater cause can at times mean taking an unpopular stance. Doing so occasionally will actually work to the benefit of the individual taking the stance. That person will be viewed as someone who is not a lackey of the administration but someone who upholds standards even in difficult times. All of these strategies portray the individual as an advocate for others and their ideas. Advocates are popular, admired, and powerful people who inspire loyalty in others. Loyalty is very important. Loyalty begets loyalty and in turn generates favors and protection.

Since perception is key, it is important to be seen as a selfless individual. Rule one in this strategy is to never advocate for oneself. As stated, it is better to advocate for others or for popular causes instead. Helping others who face the same problems will reap benefits for all, including the individual.

You Win Some, You Lose Some

It is important to realize that an individual cannot always win. The key is, as the old adage states to, "know which battles to fight." There is a time to let go and move on. Persistence is important, but continuing to fight for a lost cause will eventually result in an individual being labeled as stubborn or an obstructionist. Once this belief is institutionalize the individual will be seen as someone who is not a team player and someone with whom others cannot work. If others shy away from working with an individual then opportunities to implement policies or make changes are minimized, as is the possibility of building personal influence.

The key to deciding which battles to wage rests with understanding both the internal politics within a university and the major players who are active in these politics. Starting a war with the wrong person can be deadly.

Share The Credit

Another important method of empowerment is to always share the credit that success brings. This credit must be shared with anyone who had even the slightest part in it. Deflecting personal praise into team pride is a successful strategy that will bring big rewards later down the road. Unsolicited praise, both privately and in public, for those who helped make a project successful will make people feel good and take pride in what they have accomplished. In turn, these individuals will be willing to work even harder for their leader on the next project.

Conversely, it is just as crucial for a leader to accept responsibility for failure, providing it does not seriously impact or jeopardize a person's career in the long run. A well timed "mea culpa" can do wonders. People like to see others admit mistakes and apologize. It makes the person look human. A willingness to accept the responsibility for failure and then apologizing is very often seen as a strength, not a weakness.

Empowerment also comes from information. Whenever possible share bits of information with co-workers. People like to be in the know and in the loop. This includes sharing bits of information from the university grapevine. It even means sharing the local gossip or "dishing the dirt" at times as long as no real harmful personal information is divulged. People love to get the inside scoop about what is happening in other people's lives. A word of caution here is important. It is crucial not to share any secrets one has promised to keep. It is detrimental to be viewed as a gossip monger or worse, someone who cannot be trusted.

It is a reality that individuals like to share what they know. It demonstrates that they too have important information to share. As a result, very often even the smallest bit of shared information will bring back important information that can be very useful.

Calling In Favors

It is essential to know when to call in favors that you have built up over time. In order to do so it is important to keep an accurate record of when and for whom those favors were performed. People tend to forget obligations over time. Worse yet, they tend to believe that the favors they have performed for someone else outweigh the ones they received. An accurate reminder of just how well the "books are balanced" is often critical. It is important to periodically gently point out favors that have been performed. This reminder can come from the individual who provided the favor or from others who tell of the favors that were performed. This works to an individual's advantage when the favor eventually comes due.

Favors have a shelf life. They should be called in when they can be most effective. These include for example, times when crucial policy votes are coming to the floor, or opportunities present themselves to make needed changes, or when individuals have the opportunity to enhance their careers. Another example of when to call in a favor is when someone decides to move on and leave the university. It is usually not worth the effort to continue the obligation over a long distance or an extended period of time. It is more prudent to "cash in" the favor for immediate results before the person leaves.

Conclusions

Personal networking is crucial in developing a powerful sphere of influence within any organization including universities. In the end influence is based as much upon "who you know and who knows you" as well as what you know. Favors lay the foundation for developing close personal networking ties. These ties in turn are instrumental in building successful careers.

Chapter Thirteen

Final Thoughts

Life can be unfair at times. It appears so can working at a university.

Our universities are unfortunately a microcosm of our larger society. They mirror what occurs in the "real world." As such they are prone to the same societal and personal frailties that plague the rest of America and its working force.

While a university's mission, vision, and goals may espouse loftier ambitions, in the end, it must deal with an imperfect system that often prevents it from achieving those ideals.

Today's universities offer its faculty, staff, administrators, and key personnel the promises of advancement and personal fulfillment. Very often it cannot deliver on those promises.

At times campus policy results in the wrong person being hired. Sometimes needed ideas do not see the light of day because some individuals fear the personal impact that the change from those ideas may bring.

In life some people work harder than others, and some individuals are overworked and underappreciated. This happens on a university campus as well.

Universities with strong, competent, and compassionate leaders thrive, while those with petty dictators languish. That too is a fact.

All of these occurrences are part of the life of a university.

In the end, universities are as Charles Dickens said "...the best of times...the worst of times..." (The Quotation Page, 2011).

By and large, universities are not greedy little businesses that sacrifice the quality of education to the financial bottom line. They are not uncompassionate institutes that do not worry about their students' futures. Their offices are not filled with individuals who seek a career that will guarantee them fame and fortune. They are also not antiquated and irrelevant relics of the past.

Unfortunately, they are also not the idealized manifestation of a Socratic way of life that leads its students to truth and knowledge. Some individuals do utilize it as a vehicle for personal power and prestige. In the end that is a personal choice.

What needs to be clear above all else is that these institutions are just different; not better, not worse. As such individuals who choose to work at them must do so with clear vision, not through rose colored glasses. To believe unconditionally that sheer personal dedication and hard work will result in professional recognition and advancement is akin to believing that life will always have a Disney ending.

As jaded as it may appear, the reality is that those who choose to labor in the field of higher education must learn to use the system. Only by doing so can they create change. Only by doing so can they advance their careers. "Playing the game" when it needs to be played is not an abandonment of one's principles. It is instead a necessary strategy for survival. Those that learn this lesson early make a difference in not only their own lives, but in the lives of the students they wish to help.

Niccolo Machiavelli said that "before all else, be armed" (Brainy Quotes, 2011). To make a difference those working at today's universities must be armed with the knowledge of how the system truly functions.

They must also be willing and capable of using that knowledge when necessary.

References

Aesop. <u>Bartlett's Familiar Quotations.</u> (2007). www.online-literature. com

Allen, F. (2011). <u>www.best-quotes-poems.com</u>

Antonioni, D. "Quotes on Leadership." <u>Front Range Leadership.</u> (2010). www.dougsmithtraining.com

Aristotle. <u>Nicomachean Ethics.</u> (2011). <u>http://classics.mit.edu</u>

Block, S. "Cost of Higher Education Gets More Pricey." (2007). www. usatoday.com

Carpenter, R. (March 10, 1976). <u>Dallas Morning News</u>.

Changing Minds. "Micromanagement. (2010). http://changingminds. org

Coblit, D. (2011). <u>www.best-quotes-poems.com</u>

Communication-skills-4confidence "Leadership Skills Styles : 2 BC to 2009." (2010). www.communication-skills-4confidence.com

Dickens, C. (2011). <u>The Quotation Page</u>. www.quotationspage.com

Eisen, B. "Recession? Valet Parking Arrives." (2009). <u>http://srph.it/ aAatip</u>

Jerema, C. "Sluggish Pay For American University Presidents." (2010).

http:oncampus.macleans.ca

Kettering, C. (2011). www.best-quotes-poems.com

Lewin, K, Lippitt, R., and White, R. "Leadership and Group Life." (2010). http://faculty.css.edu

Machiavelli, N. Bartlett's Familiar Quotations. (2007). www.online-literature.com

Machiavelli, N. (2011). Brainy Quotes. http://brainyquotes.com

Mizner, W. In The Colombia World of Quotations, (1996). New York: Columbia University Press.

Parada, C. Genealogical Guide to Greek Mythology. (2007). www.homepage.mac.com

Plato. The Republic. 360 B.C. (2007). http://classics.mit.edu

Proverbs. King James Bible. (2007). http://etext.lib.virginia.edu

Salaries Rise in Down Economy." (2009). www.usatoday.com

Salcedo, J. "Bureaucracy Quotes." (2010). http://thinkexist.com

Summer, G. (2011). www.best-quotes-poems.com

The Digest of Education Statistics. (2009). http://nces.ed.gov

Tuccinardi, R. Encyclopedia Mythica. (2007). www.pantheon.org

United States Department of Education. (2001). www.ed.gov

University of Colorado at Denver. "UCD Research Dollars Hit A Record $374 Million For FY 2006." (2007). www.uchsc.edu

Walton, S. "Famous Leadership Quotes." (2010). www.buzzle.com

White Stag Leadership Development. "Sharing Leadership." (2010). www.whitestag.org

Wieberg, S. Upton, J., Perez, A., Berkowitz, S. "College Football Coaches See Salaries Rise in Down Economy." (2009). www.usatoday.com